ONE HAPPY THOUGHT AT A TIME

THE Journal

Cover Design & Layout: Yetunde Shorters
www.yetundeshorters.com

For information regarding special discounts for bulk purchases of this book, for charitable donation, or for speaking engagements, please visit www.rochellegapere.com
ISBN: ISBN 978-1-7320360-1-7
Published by Rochelle Gapere
Printed in the United States of America

ONE

HAPPY THOUGHT

AT A TIME

THE *Journal*

These happy thoughts belong to

____

Learn to make happiness enhancing decisions!

How will you make happiness your priority going forward?

-Rochelle Gapere

Are you preparing for what you are wishing or hoping for?

Start preparing for what you are wishing and hoping for, so that when the time comes, you will be ready and equipped to rise to the occasion!

–Rochelle Gapere

Would 8-year-old you be proud of your current life?

–Rochelle Gapere

Is it worth giving them your joy?

It is pretty simple math, the less joy we have in our lives, the less happy we will be. The more joy we have in our lives, the happier we will be. So protect your joy and protect it fiercely!

–Rochelle Gapere

Do something today that makes your heart overflow with happiness.

When was the last time you did something that made your heart overflow with happiness?

–Rochelle Gapere

Be grateful for your portion in life!

–Rochelle Gapere

Grateful that God woke me up this morning. He didn't have to, but He did. And for that, I am beyond thankful!

-Rochelle Gapere

Maybe it's not working out the way you think it should because God wants to exceed your expectations.

–Rochelle Gapere

You honor yourself when
you treat yourself well.
And you should.

–Rochelle Gapere

Focus on your blessings more than your problems!

-Rochelle Gapere

Don't get sidetracked by negativity and miss the great things God is about to do in your life.

Be extremely protective and cognizant of who and what you allow in your space. Energy is contagious!

–Rochelle Gapere

Stop imagining the worst case scenario and use that energy to imagine the BEST case scenario.

What's the BEST that could happen today?

–Rochelle Gapere

Do not allow fear to hold you hostage. One brave decision can change your entire life for the better.

–Rochelle Gapere

Protect yourself from emotionally draining interactions by putting buffers in place to preserve your happiness!

–Rochelle Gapere

Imagine your life 15 years from now! Are you living your life right now in alignment with how you imagine yourself?

There is power in purposeful living.

And the power is yours!

–Rochelle Gapere

Be kind to yourself!
Everyone makes mistakes!

–Rochelle Gapere

There is supreme power in deliberately tailoring the messaging that infiltrates your thoughts on a daily basis! What can your mind use less of? Try doing away with it and replacing those thoughts with better ones!

–Rochelle Gapere

There are more than enough resources on this earth for all of us to enjoy and share, we just have to let go of little and think limitless.

How can you take the limits off your thoughts today?

–Rochelle Gapere

God is not a one hit wonder. If He did it before, He can certainly do it again.

–Rochelle Gapere

While you have life: live it fully, tell & show your loved ones how much you love them, and deflect all bad vibes.

–Rochelle Gapere

You are the architect of your own future. If you are not happy with your current situation,

change it now!

–Rochelle Gapere

Every storm runs out of rain
and the sun will
eventually shine again.

–Rochelle Gapere

Fight for YOUR happiness, and WIN!

How will you fight for your happiness and strengthen your happiness muscles to win?

–Rochelle Gapere

When life isn't going your way, do you think God is punishing you?

–Rochelle Gapere

What do YOU want? Until you get clear about what you want, you will keep attracting experiences or people counter to your desire.

–Rochelle Gapere

Not everyone can go where God is taking you. Be comfortable with that fact. Season. Reason. Lifetime.

Adjust accordingly.

–Rochelle Gapere

Don't let your past delay your destiny.

We are wiser because of the total sum of our experiences, both good and bad. If we want to be happy we have to let go of what's gone, be grateful for what remains, and look forward to what is coming.

–Rochelle Gapere

Happiness

is

Kindness

–Rochelle Gapere

Stop postponing your happiness for a later date. There is no time like the present to do the things that make you happy.

Life is too unpredictable to hold your happiness hostage!

–Rochelle Gapere

There is no lack of happiness. Happiness is infinite. You can have happiness today and happiness tomorrow and the day after and the day after that.

–Rochelle Gapere

We never know where life will take us, or who we will meet along the journey. If we open our hearts with love and kindness to new people and new experiences, the journey will lay pleasant surprises in our path.

–Rochelle Gapere

God can do anything, you know—far more than you could ever imagine or guess or request in your wildest dreams!

–Ephesians 3:20

You have the power to choose one happy thought every day, one happy thought every hour, or one happy thought every minute! The more happy thoughts you choose, I guarantee the result will be a happier you!

–Rochelle Gapere

LET'S CONNECT ON SOCIAL MEDIA

Facebook
www.facebook.com/rochelle.gapere

Instagram
www.instagram.com/rochelle.gapere

Twitter
www.twitter.com/rochellegapere

LinkedIn
www.linkedin.com/in/rochelle-gapere

Website
www.rochellegapere.com

Made in the USA
Middletown, DE
25 April 2023